THE ZEN OF FALLING LEAVES

POEMS BY ANGEL ELISA COLLIER

BLUE LIGHT PRESS ◆ 1ST WORLD PUBLISHING

1ˢᵗ WORLD
PUBLISHING

SAN FRANCISCO ◆ FAIRFIELD ◆ DELHI

THE ZEN OF FALLING LEAVES

Copyright ©2016 by Angel Elisa Collier

1st World Library
PO Box 2211
Fairfield, IA 52556
www.1stworldpublishing.com

Blue Light Press
www.bluelightpress.com
Email: bluelightpress@aol.com

Book & Cover Design
Melanie Gendron
www.melaniegendron.com

Cover Art
"Morning Light" by Melanie Gendron

First Edition

Library of Congress Control Number: 2016937043

ISBN 9781421837536

ACKNOWLEDGEMENTS

Heartfelt appreciation to Diane Frank for her instruction, guidance and assistance in making this book possible. Special thanks to JoLynn Gates, Melanie Gendron, Lisha Adela Garcia, Betsy Snider, Lynne Barnes, Ken Pobo, KB Ballentine and Laura Stamps.

Dedicated to the loving memory of my parents,
Frank S. Gallay and Mary M. Gallay

CONTENTS

Arabesque

The flurry of autumn
spins on little squirrel toes,
as acorns toss their berets into the wind.
Flames break from the blaze
sweeping across parchment of sky,
swirling around my ankles,
sinking into the wet, brown earth of my eyes,
crackling under my feet.

Rotting berries, old rain,
carcass of leaves
lift their fumes from the damp earth
like a fog.
Spiders weave dreamcatchers in the October wind.
This moment dangles at the end of a branch,
soft, ripe, as I drink its wine.
While footprints stitch the spiced woods,
I believe in the compass of my feet.

The mandarin sun slowly lifts its slice.
Fingers of sunlight
stained with the blood of raspberries,
touch the lacquered countryside
of cinnamon, amber and candy apple leaves.

A tiny cloud surrenders to gravity,
raindrops veiled within the ivory
fog of her haunches.
Beneath the pine tree,
shimmer of fur inside rising light.
Sapphire eyes follow a ballerina
pirouetting in the wind,

floating red,
softly
downward.
As the eyelid of sky begins to close,
stars appear across my skin.
Ice fills the rivers inside red maple leaves.
I'm harvesting feathers from migrating geese
for my dreams,
as shadows flood the hills with secrets.

Trees reach into moonlight
with bones of longing.
I fold velvet limbs of fur into my heartbeat,
my slow breath fills the cave
with wild blueberry perfume,
as the sun rotates around my winter dreams
of spawning salmon under a waterfall.

November

Across forty acres of rented Earth
I unravel the flannel threads of my cocoon,
unfolding powdered wings splattered with leopard spots,
fluttering through the cool liniment of silence
as the clenched bones of my soul
relax into water.

Empty walnut shells
scatter along the crisp, brown tile of fallen leaves.
Boots breeding miles,
soul deep in the wet, musty smell of death.

Crow tacks his announcements
onto the silver bulletin board of the landscape.
Flicker sips cider from a sweet, rotting apple
that still clings to the bones of its mother.

Below the wispy, white hair of cirrus clouds,
a garland of three hawks
navigates around my heart.
Blue jay shatters the silence
beyond a pine-spackled hill.
Childhood dreams slowly fade,
curl and scrape each other,
shivering into my ear
from the furrowed throat of an oak tree.

As time collapses backward
into the soft, black fur of night,
skeletons of trees
tangle into each other's lives.

Another November morning
slowly opens a stiff, pink eye
across the shimmering blue mirror.
I look beyond the raspberry ripples,
the watery trees
and frogs leaping between clouds.
Among them all,
I find myself.

In This Moment

Inspired by the poem "Now" by Laura Stamps

Early February
and the moments flutter like snowflakes,
blurring the frost-bitten cheek of sky,
each minute a frozen imprint on the Earth.
If only my life could be knitted and purled
from fleeting moments of bliss,
to be worn only in the present.
Shimmering hexagons cut from the wool of clouds
into a quilt, milk-white and sun-dappled,
translucent as crystal,
a tern's wing
fluttering across my dreams,
stitched together with the silver thread of peace.
Time snows at my feet,
reflecting the white fire of heaven.

THE TAO OF MORNING

The sky removes its velvet nightgown.
The oriole sun rises from its nest
scattering orange feathers across the hills,
lifting into lilac petals of sky.

I backstroke out of the seafoam waters of a dream
as hope dares to open its wings,
allowing the chill of the east wind
and whatever happens today,
to breathe through me.

Sparkling bird songs
from grosbeak, house wren,
purple finch,
thread tree branches with spun sugar.
Ginger tabby rolls into a belly dance on her back,
waiting for the sweet cream of love
to pour from my hand.
Chittering squirrel grips higher truths
with needled toes,
holding me with an innocent stare.

The heaviness within me
leaves deep footprints
at the edge of a forgotten place.
But when I look behind my left shoulder,
sunlight casting its net across a meadow of dew,
a thousand rainbows explode into my eyes.
Each one an answered prayer.
The miracle of this morning
wrapping soft ribbons of light
around my spirit.

Forest of the Ice Queen

New snow forms a crust
over whiskers of a cat's dream.
The sun peeks through ruffled lace
of winter sky,
fluttering his fiery lashes
on the enameled shoulders of a birch tree,
unable to make her thaw.

Her translucent skin
sparkles in his light.
She blows an icy kiss into the clouds,
rattling pearls inside a north wind.
From a veined branch,
a cardinal drapes her ring finger.
The cherry of her spring
hangs suspended from a crystal corset.

WALKING THROUGH WINTER TREES

Below the ligaments of my wandering soul,
the thorns of ice flowers
prick the pebbles of my feet.
My eyes swallow the stars
while January etches ferns
against crystal panes.

Above the burial ground
of dead birds, squirrels and last summer's wildflowers,
toe points toward the rattle of shivering bones.
Stepping over fallen birch,
I hear the crack of snow
as my foot reconnects with gravity
and the iron ore of grief.

Lactating sky
folds into ivory reeds
between skeletons of trees.
Under a thin moon,
white lace sighs on arthritic branches
between evergreen spires
where I kneel.

While the earth carries my burdens,
my woolen hands reach for the arms of trees,
their brittle fingers
vying to touch my shoulder.
As my eyes graze across the blue tracks behind me,
I know I am following my dreams.

FEATHERS

A cardinal opens his carmine feathers
across the eastern horizon,
miles above the viridian hills of my sighs.
His morning aria threads sunbeams
over my eyes
as I hear the lift and fall of wings
through the phosphorescence.
I watch koi swim across the rippling sky
and a chickadee sipping pearls
off a pine needle.

A snowy egret opens her fan like a geisha,
fluttering across the blushing cheek
of early morning sky.
I can only watch from behind a bone cage
as she fades into citrus clouds.

Translucent wings fold over my eyes,
a forest of shivering trees looming over me.
An easterly wind
tousles my hair with sonnets.
Why do I suddenly long
to be in my mother's eyes?

The trees are singing to angels,
their songs like messages
in green bottles thrown across the sea.
Orioles bloom like sunflowers across the cerulean sky.
Tiny bells shower from a rose-breasted grosbeak,
the weight of yearning
held up by the sinewy biceps of an oak tree.
Children fly out of blue eggs.

The rapid flutter of wings
shakes the nest like the slam of a door.

The north wind snaps its cat teeth
through the puffed body of a chickadee.
Undaunted, her piccolo skips along
like a Mozart symphony,
perched on the capillary of my emotions.
If only my feet lingered
inside winter's white light
oblivious to the needled winds of gossip,
they would be dancing a minuet,
leaving their gentle bird tracks in the snow.

Early Spring

I.

As I rise out of the earth
of my mother's uterus,
how can I enter this world without screaming?
Slender, broken spines
across an echo of human footprints.
Faces scattered into the forgotten.

Feathered leaves ruffle my shoulders.
Green bones reach across the shadows,
wading in pools of blinding gold.
Soft, white shell
too small to contain me,
windswept kisses blow open my petals,
exposing light.
Trickled dew over a blushing petal
where I'm missing the bumblebee.
The monarch comforts me
under the stained-glass window of his wings.
From shimmering ruby,
a hummingbird wants to touch me
from the inside out.

II.

As the sky unbuttons its fleece,
dawn wraps candy-apple scarves
around the chilled shoulders of the landscape.
Fire ignites the meadow of my eyes.
My frozen dreams begin to thaw.
Thoughts shagged with ice

glisten in sunlight,
ideas trickle like a fountain into a pool of verse.
The fertile womb below my feet
sprouts a new book of hymns.
I listen to the trees sing love songs
releasing their wings into the flames.

GRACKLE

Metallic silver slowly ages into amber
along the edges of my memories.
Black and white images brittle through time
like old bones,
and crease along familiar limbs and faces
as they unfold from remembering.
If the camera knows the secret to immortality,
why does morning dew linger on the hollyhock
long into afternoon?

I try to escape through an open window,
until a grackle appears at the bird bath
in the wooded backyard of my eyes.
Clothespin feet grip the marbled edge of his life.
Still as a garden gnome,
the fire of his eyes loses oxygen
focused on the other side of the horizon.
The vulgar lyrics of his youth
bellowed under a black scowl,
are silenced from teeth marks near his throat.
He fought the lioness of death
for a few more moments of rustling aspen.

With crippled wings,
I oar my boat across the grass.
Its iridescent shimmer of indigo, violet and green
makes even dying beautiful.
The soft nest where I used to speak
only rattles now,
but nobody hears me.
My only companions are a muttering redwing blackbird
and a heather-brown rabbit

too busy eating the shadow of a pear tree to notice.
As the sky furrows its brow,
I pull the dark veil across my body.

I watch him drain through the cracks,
fingers of emerging sunlight
stroke his collapsed head.
For a brief moment, the trees stood silent.
I hold his limp body behind my ribcage,
allowing the wisdom of this moment
to change the size of my pupils.
Like the echo of dawn leaping
victorious over the dark wing of night,
two bunnies still wet from birth
vault over death
as though it were a toy.

An elbow of grackles
glissade across the blue ice of sky
through floating snow banks.
A long arm opens into an embrace
to receive its newest co-pilot
migrating home.

The Translucent Forest

The weight of beauty
arcs its enameled spine with icicle chandeliers,
illuminating the spired chapel of the woods.
Milky wafers crack under the rubber soles of intrusion.
A red nightshade berry swaddled in ice,
drapes the end of a purled branch.
Above the tinseled clouds of my breath,
a honeycomb of glass
laminates this fragile other-world.

As the breeze rises,
ice clicks on the trees like wind chimes
through the stiff silence.
Rainbows swirl around crystal shells
that fall like piano notes on crusted snow,
shattering like glass
as sunbeams lean against the trees
and tears of joy freeze into pearls.

A mirror beveled between hard snow
and arthritic trees
says nothing,
reflecting only silver lanterns
shimmering in the ice-blue sky.

WILD HORSES

The blue mare gallops
across the watery pasture
and floating mountains,
bobbing through kelp,
sipping moonlight.
Corralled only where Neptune drapes
the shoulders of Gaea,
chameleon eyes study me,
one at a time.
Her tail whorls into a cockleshell
around a blade of sea grass.
Rings of bone
jut under translucent parchment skin.
Early dawn unfurls raspberry streamers
along the rippled shore.
As she holds her pregnant husband
with both eyes,
they blush green, mottled orange,
scarlet.
Holding tails,
they ascend snout-to-snout
out of the coral reefs,
spiraling into cerulean ocean of sky.

Echoes On The Water

Old growth wisdom
leads me into the river,
my soul free of starched robes.
Moon head moppet clutching a starfish
reclines on the sleek, wet log of his back.
White feathers in the periwinkle sky
stretch across sunlight.
An otter swivels and dives into rippled sky
through the foaming billows of his playground.

When I look at him,
I am five years old again.
Diving under a waterfall of pearls
he bends streamers of amber light,
etching lithographs on stone.
Sharp clicks hammer through the roar,
two halves of a clamshell
shatter on a lump of rock.

Husband and wife
roll over in a blue, ruffled quilt.
Napping on a mattress of kelp,
paws clasp in the vortex.
Crescendo of rings are the silver echoes
of their laughter.

BUMBLEBEE

A beauty mark
across the petaled cheek of my backyard.
Wildflowers hang their lace
under buzzing sunlight.
A meadowlark composes a song this morning
as I unfurl into the marbled sky,
reaching for truth.
You stumble over a pearl of dew,
sipping nectar from my hand.

Liquid light flows out of your body
inside the hollow oak tree,
knitting honey pots
from the sticky yarn of daffodils.

You hover over the marigolds of my childhood.
Warm, southern wind of my thoughts
flutters the ruffled coils of your universe
along the lake's edge.
The memory crystallized
inside a glass, hexagon jar.

As you land on the lilac-scented edges of my heart,
sunlight shatters the isinglass windows
of your wings.
Your wisdom sticks to my soul.
As you fly out of my eyes,
I feel the sting of your absence.

Afternoon In The Country

Keeping pace only with myself
through the smog,
gunfire shatters the crystal windows of my eyes.
The steel arrogance of corporate monoliths
obstructs my view of the trees.

Floating on a pair of metal wings,
I watch the hologram of corn, wheat and wild fields
rustle their skirts in a wind dance.
Sunflower petals cover my eyes
as I rent a patch of blue sky.
Horses lap the warm, melted butter of sunlight.
The cool breath of spring
carries the wild scent of hay and musk.
Windblown daydreams
funnel under my sunhat.

Long after woodpeckers have flown
with their hammers and chisels,
dark windows penetrate
the bones of a dead tree.

The corn rises out of the earth's uterus,
gazing over the soft edges of her abdomen,
stretching mantis-green fingers into the sky
as if for some higher purpose.

Voices inside trees
etch the soft daylily hours of afternoon.
My eyes paddle the landscape,
sea-foam grass rolls onto a beach
of dandelions and clover.

A cow licks the honey of my emotions
from my fingers.
Our eyes make conversation
beneath the white-crested ocean of sky
as I'm corralled by hooves.
A heavy sigh from the pines
lifts the warm clouds of their breathing
into colors of the day.

The crisp, candy air of spring
wafts through the lace curtains of my childhood.
I shudder with laughter.

I watch a meadowlark shatter the porcelain sky
on his way home.
I sleep with violets blooming in my hair.

Planting seeds of happiness,
my fingers become tangled roots
under a rotating sky.
I grow wild with nectar.
Coral petals bloom
where I lose all desire to speak.

In Praise of Nectarines

Dawn is ripe on the horizon,
a melody of photons
beaming through the bunting blue sky.
If I am still,
I can almost hear the sun
lift above the pines.
In my kitchen,
I squeeze juice out of a blue porcelain bowl
onto the countryside
bathed in marigold glow.
Rivers of candy apple red
burnt orange and lemonade,
pool across the eastern shores of my dreaming.
I pluck hope from its stem,
and hold the colors of the day in my hand.
I feel the wild shape of hunger
in the branches of my fingers.
As I bite into this moment,
sunlight spills out of an open window.
Its meadow lark syrup sticks to my soul.

Mountain Spirit

Under the eyelid of midnight,
winter stars shower
over the high cheekbones of Tibet.
Twenty thousand feet
above the ice clouds of my breathing,
a snow leopard bends over her sacrifice
on a jagged altar. Hunger moans,
dragging wool three times her weight
between breaths, up vertical walls
dappled with pines, broken shale
and crusted snow.

Black roses bloom
through your body of beige fur.
White shawls of mist
wrap around the mountains of your shoulders.
You carry the silence of your large paws
across glazed mountain peaks.

Love at first sight.
Sapphire mirrors shatter
through a curtain of falling snow.
How serene you look camouflaged
between snowflakes and rippled rock.
You yawn and stretch
all over my curiosity.
A mottled secret swaggers over the peak
like something out of Chinese mythology.

Beyond the snow goose feathers of my dream
ten thousand jagged steps below,
a Buddhist monk bends his knees,
prayers spin in his hand.
The wind carries the breath of rhododendrons
to the peaks.
Tiny bells fracture the silence
that weighs more than a snow leopard's stare.

One set of paw prints leads west,
where snow melts on the stepping stones
into the blue eye of God.

THE SIXTH OCEAN

You've leaked out of a floating pearl
when Earth was white,
melting into yourself,
filling deep bays under high, rocky cliffs.
White birches, pine trees and lighthouses
circle a wolf's head,
his green eye looking out
from an island of coniferous trees.

Desperation throws down a rope
as I struggle to climb out of everyone's eyes.
Below the bobbing feathers of a seagull's dream,
crystal green walls roll down
across the jagged rocks of my worries,
burnishing the sharp edges into emeralds.

I want to dive into your bones
through the skin of desperate fingers,
feeling the barnacles of ice
between my shoulder blades.
But I can only watch you
flow through the jail bars of my hands
until my fingertips shrivel.

I pull the sun across my shoulders
like a flaxen shawl.
But the longer I stay near you,
the more I tremble.

I see an open wound
where sky breaks away
from the rippled edge of your skin

and seagulls enter.
Where pink clouds fall,
you disappear
beyond an eagle's telescope.

Under the REM of shifting sky,
all the stars have fallen into your lap.
White flames rush to shore
beneath the Leaf Falling Moon.

Glass angels pour golden light
out of themselves
through the porcelain bell of sky.
At the edge of a blue continent,
I shrink into the moss.
Only my shadow grows legs.

Beneath the spotted wings of a hawk,
you leap onto the rocky shores of my emotions.
Filling your lungs with north wind,
you lift into sky.
White swans rest on the edge of your breath
before their feathers scatter
upon the hungry molars of the shore.
Jade glows in sunlight
before it shatters like glass.
How could I possibly lower my eyes
just to blink?

Inside the sun of an eagle's eye,
bowls of wild aster
fill with golden light,
early frost sparkles along stairways of stone,
and happiness melts into its bones.

As I walk away from you,
with every step
the plaited cord narrows and tightens
until it snaps,
and I take to bleeding inwardly.

Finding My Center

As windswept trees brush
the sky's pale, amethyst hair,
I lay my head
on the feathered lap of the meadow.
Clover blooms around my temples.
Dreams ignite with the yellow fire of honeybees.
I spin elliptical orbits around my sky,
grass stains across the knees of my spirit.

The sun offers its golden wafer
upon the altar of a cumulus cloud,
the daily liturgy vibrates
with the chanting of a rose breasted grosbeak.
I follow my breath
to the rhythm of a cow's meditation.
Shivering aspens murmur psalms
throughout another sacred day.

Hymns fly out of the fluttering leaves of my mouth.
With feet sprouting roots in the earth,
the branches of my arms
reach for the light.
Through the mist splattered with wet pearls,
the memory of my parents' love
is heaven's compass.

Rhapsody Of Silence

The year grows white with age.
I lift my tongue
to the udder of sky.
A confetti of honeymooners
drape my window with their negligee.
I listen to snowflakes breathe upon the hills.
Bell sleeves and iridescent wings
sprout on fronds of spruce, balsam and fir.

Hickory branches tinseled with ice
weave their brittle fingers through a cirrus cloud.
Snowshoes waffle the landscape.
Only the loud crack from a poplar tree
deepens the silence.

Where guardian angels are made,
snow-caked mittens grip around
green wooden slots of childhood dreams.
Metal runners cut through flying snow
and echoes of laughter.
A woman in an apron
fills an empty doorway with breath clouds
that summon a warm kitchen,
hot Ovaltine,
and a lap blanket with a pulse.

My frost-bitten dreams
thaw under the breath of a snow leopard.
...A muffled howl through the trees
and I awake with Raggedy Ann.

I pause to hear the wind talk.
The red barn defies its knife-edged words.
A light switch in the horizon
spills vermilion ink
into the backdrop of a log cabin,
smoking its brick pipe into the night.
The boreal lion bares his teeth
from the edge of a roof.
Over a quilt of fallen stars,
silken veils of amber, violet, opal and rose
swirl across the black wing of midnight.

As the sun wakes from hibernation,
a tiny drop of water
falls from the eye of a snowman.

HEIDI

From her starched and buckled limbs,
she runs into the arms of a northwest wind,
shaking down the leaves.
Peter lifts his head above the sheep.
Honeybees dart out of the golden petals of her braids
blooming into a waving field of sunflowers.
She picks edelweiss
until her tiny fingers grow wild with hummingbirds.

Under the silent migration of cumulus clouds,
goat bells shake across the pink heather.
Between the mountains and feathered pines,
a shimmering ribbon of glass
from a schoolgirl's daydream
mirrors the rippling sky.
A distant yodel
is the only voice to answer.

The Alps rise over blue fire,
their jagged calves burn
in a wild garden of gentians and bellflowers.
The sun drapes a yellow shawl
across its cascading shoulders,
emptying the dark, bristled pockets with pine trees.
Its ruffled face cuts the sky
into a jigsaw puzzle.
Heidi climbs its ridged back with desperate eyes
that fill with snow,
to watch angels pray on the summit.

Grandfather's voice rumbles
across the slow, dark boil of sky,
its sulphur reaching over the geometric edges
of her tranquility.
His chalet cleaves into the pines
like a swallow's nest that disappears
inside the shadow of a thunderstorm.
The scent of thick, warm bread and toasted cheese
floats across layers of candlelight,
soft voices folding into prayer.

Clouds gather around her mouth
in the chilled moonlight.
As she sinks into hay and quilted dreams,
Orion slowly disappears.

Sunlight Through Curtains

Early June,
the morning sun rises out of its nest,
oriole feathers touching angels.
The bur oak is a kaleidoscope,
its shiny mirrors dapple the bedroom floor
with lemon drops and other-worldly creatures.
The cardinal opens his red petals with a serenade.
As the warmth of anticipation rises in me,
I am filled with light.

After Froot Loops, I change my sky,
climbing into kitchen cupboards and bedroom closets
with Pinnocchio the cat,
pulling stars out of cracks.
The soft flannel of darkness
drapes over my folded limbs
that burrow like eclipsed moons
among newspaper and shopping bags.

The silkweed floss of her touch,
the apron and brush of iodine
over scraped emotions,
are the ripples of light
flickering on the water,
cascading over me
in a baptism of divine Mother Love.
As I feel the translucent wings of a west wind,
the light expands through the open door.

The dove's melted psalms of peace
chisel the lonely stillness of late morning.
I wander through scraps of forest

constructing a fortress of daydreams
with log chairs, oak leaf curtains,
barricades of poison ivy.

At the edge of a deep green mystery,
I run through the yellow fire of sunlight
pitching a Frisbee,
cartwheeling over a Crayola of wildflowers,
reaching the souls of birds
from a tire swing.

The afternoon sun percolates
through filters of spun sugar
glazing the blueberry sky,
wrapping a bright green scarf
around the shoulders of our backyard,
stippling the pleats of a robin's skirt
as he sunbathes over a small, crumbled, cement patch
outside my bedroom window.

As crickets drum against the soft hide of evening,
the breath of prayer leads me
toward the quiet end of our street
where only trees and squirrels grow.
Thoughts too serious for a child
are my walking cane.
As I ride my bike inside the wind,
arms of dreams reach out to me
from the center of a full moon.
The voice of lullabies
is calling me home.

THE RED PIANO

Behind the warm smile of sunlit curtains
bathed in the lemonade glow of daydreams,
shapes of light dribble over a bassinet of dolls,
splashing across the yellow ochre floor.
Where rose-scented secrets
are locked behind stucco walls,
her fingers try to reach the soft edges of memory.

Under the red wing of a Schoenhut piano,
birdsongs weave around the soft bones of tentative hands,
seashells over the treble clef.
She runs out of keys before the end of a song,
like words of a conversation
with a pretend friend.
The Beatles try to hold her hand
across the keybord.
For three minutes,
her name is Michelle.

Soft paws of a child knead its spine
until the music shivers,
until it rubs against the heart,
purring.

THE ZEN MASTER

Across the long snore of twilight,
my cat Mila laps moon milk
from her marbled shoulder.
An hour before the sky lifts its heavy eyelid,
I watch a shooting star,
dusty dreams fading into sunrise.
The weight of silence leans into my bones,
even as the first robin clears his throat.

Tumbling among flannel roses,
I open the ivory brocades of my eyes,
eager to unwrap the shining, yellow gift of today.

Wet stars evaporate
on the open petals of violet sky.
Her limber patience
stretches across muted light,
soft button of her paw
under the bedroom door.
I taste the first sugary bites of lemon meringue hours
and begin the day with laughter,
ankles attacked by kitty slippers.
She doesn't notice my wild, punk, pillow hair.
She's too busy scraping skin off my arms
with the loofah sponge of her tongue.

Amber eyes unmoving.
She yawns over my words,
shedding what is unimportant.
Lapping up the sweet cream of the moment,
the soft seashells of her feet
tell me here and now is all that purrs,

as she wraps a plush tail
around my heart.

As silver flowers bloom
across the midnight sky,
she folds into herself,
a plump spool of cat dreams
floating across the soft fur of night
connecting stars,
finding God behind the third eyelid.

Black Angel

A shadow waddles
across the catwalk of my kitchen floor
modeling a pair of ebony bloomers.
From an unearthly yowl,
air molecules tremble and explode,
crashing over my equanimity.
The yellow shards of morning
in fragments on my hardwood floor.
Nettled paws bat my resistance.
Her glare fires telepathic commands for chicken.

Leaves that flicker
to the winds of her thoughts,
fold against her head.
The nimbus clouds of her eyes
hover over the trapeze artist in a silver dress
balancing across the telephone cable.

Warm milk sighs
into the soft, black purse of her mouth.
Feathered paws knead the sinewed
shoulders
of Earth.
From the soft cello of her throat,
she vibrates through my fingers
then arcs into a yoga bath.
She draws the sun across her body,
silk chocolate shimmering out of darkness.
She whorls into her heartbeat with a sigh,
emeralds rolling back into a dream.

An azalea petal blooms from her mouth,
salivating with dew.
It sweeps over my temple, cheek and ear
like sandpaper
till I shudder.

I inhale the last lingering scent of patchouli
from an empty sweater,
as if it were my mother come back to life.
Two swirling ponds of emotion
look back at me.
Something trickles down my cheek,
and evaporates under her breath.

For JuJu

I.

She sheds her fur
all over my authority,
teeth marks
in every piece of cellophane in the house.
Faking sleep, I feel the nudge of her white glove.
Only when she hears me floating
through the translucent meadow of a dream,
rustling between pink linen geraniums,
she welcomes me back to Earth
with a hungry sigh.

She wobbles across my back
on the mottled berries of her toes.
A song rumbles in my ear
from the soft paws of her breathing,
until I shiver.

As Monday morning sky
frowns with thoughts of rain,
their scissored words
burrow between my shoulders.
With my back to the bathroom wall,
courage breaks at the knees.
She looks inside me,
honest as a cardinal's ardent song.
I feel the silk threads of a milkweed pod
tap my cheek
as she holds me
inside the olive fields of her eyes.

When I watch her attack sunbeams
and empty paper bags on the kitchen floor,
now is all that breathes.

II.

November shakes like an old man,
lifting a trembling, bony branch
out of its wrinkled trunk
into the white hair of sky.
The stratosphere, stiff and cold,
as when my brother found you
sprawled on the floor.

You loved high places,
climbing over kitchen cabinets
as if they were clouds to heaven,
finally reaching the summit,
into the Lap of God.

EMBROIDERED LILIES

"A pair of bound lilies
means a big urn of tears."
. . . ancient Chinese proverb

Slanted mischief
flickers above the mountains of your cheekbones.
Feet disappear in a wind tunnel,
lifting you over the rice fields
like the swift legs of a gazelle.
You wear the silk robe of sunlight across your bare arms.

While maple trees empty their pockets of rubies,
you bury perfect, little toes
in the cool, peony garden.
A stranger approaching the gate
with hardware and strips of cotton.
Your tiny, six-year-old feet
bolt for the gazelles.

The break of an arch
becomes the eulogy of your childhood.
Only your screams escape
through the paper lattice window.
Curled, broken toes
dig into your soul,
crescent moons dangle
in the night sky of silk slippers.

A rainbow of embroidered lilies
hides the gangrene of your wings.
But you smile for your husband
as he admires the red silk and lotus designs,
while you teeter.

As you roll the opium paste into a pellet,
roast it over the fire
and offer him the pipe,
you realize dreams do not walk through compound walls.

Women will bind themselves long after 1912,
when you trade your lotus shoes
for stilettos
and laminate your face
for another Chinese New Year.

House of Escher

How did I wake up on the sleeping escalator
where every tone is false?
Stone pillars and slabs of arched granite
ornament the architecture
which I am forced to inhabit.
Half-moon windows reveal nothing inside.

Faceless clones
parade on an orbital staircase,
circumnavigating the void
in the middle of this Escher lithograph.
With no exit or destination,
they must run on self-recharging batteries.

People watcher on the third floor,
are you the boss? Get a dog!

This gravity well halts my escape.
A vireo caged inside a broken piano
hovers in her own stratosphere,
living on crumbs of her dreams.

WALLS

A medieval fortress
wraps itself around rose-scented secrets.
An edifice of jutting sandstones
thwarts a mouthful of arrows.

A monolith of oak trees
become camouflage.
I linger behind the grandiflora bush
until yelping teenage boys from a pick-up
pass me by.
I slip on my Greta Garbo eyes.

A smirk, a shifty eye,
venomous spider weaving messages on the office wall.
Monkeys squat on my desk
reminding me what to do with my hands.

Flanks of plaster and concrete
stretch through memories of flight,
always reaching for wings,
frustrated by gravity.

Two-dimensional Japanese gardens,
flat warblers and paper trees
help me forget I have walls.

INFECTED WINDS

Why do your eyes only face outward?
As mouths pull back across the office,
she feels your teeth
arrow between her shoulder blades,
as she tries to take another step toward sunset.

Guilty for trespassing under the same clouds,
an empty purse
defends her presence.
As the fissure near her spine deepens,
can you see your reflection
in the russet shimmer of her eyes?

As tabloids spin in your knitting circles,
how long will it take
before the truth weighs more than your tongue?

INNER VOICE

The sky opens its fluted shell,
the pearl of a new day
shimmers from an abalone cave.
Velvet heart petals open in gratitude.
The dove's liquid pathetique
saturates me with peace.

May I always listen
to the soft wind chime of my heart's desire,
leaving its echoes
across silver leaves of moonlight,
gardenia candles,
the silent chatter of my books
waiting to be held,
reverberating over wings of snow geese
where I dream.

Along the black and white river
of a Chopin nocturne,
the hushed secrets beneath my pen
spill my water bowl of colors
onto the canvas of my strongest voice.
To live my life
sailing on the rugged boat
across the ocean of my name.

As human tongues spit their nails,
my life hangs on a cross
until my spirit breaks free
into the arms of trees,
clearing the throat of my inner voice,
a mirror to the Divine.

CHERRY MOON

When the translucent shells of your eyes opened
after dreaming between your mother's hips,
a meteor shower of cherries
exploded over the hills
through the warm, starched air of August.

Mink eyes tell the world only what matters,
but the cherry wood skin stretched
across the mountains of your cheeks,
reveals all your ancestors
who lived and died with the smoke,
when you could hear the breath
of two hundred million buffaloes on the prairie,
when even babies were warriors.

The red rivers below your skin
surge with the memory of Crazy Horse.
Your cells connect like stars,
the constellations of a heyoka
dancing backwards.

Sage burns in an abalone shell.
Fire burns inside you.
Spotted eagle feathers flutter in your hair,
a raptor inside the turtle shell
where heavy stones glow red
in the crow wing of night.
Your heart beats out of an elk drum.
With a voice like black coffee,
ancient Lakota songs spill hot from your lungs.
Sweat, water and steam
shapeshift into spirits.

Tobacco prayers murmur silently
as you feel the earth's weight
in salt water.

Still pulling shrapnel out of your leg
forty years after Vietnam,
no one hears you scream.

The sun smokes your eyes.
The drummer's wail
keeps your beaded moccasins dancing in circles
around the cottonwood tree
where you hang by a rope.
You drag the grieving widow and town drunk
out of the fire in your chest.
You carry their burdens inside your scars.

You are the wild horse.
The wind is your motorcycle.
The place you call home is under a black Stetson
where all your secrets hide.

You pray through a cedar flute in the cathedral,
psalms of peace floating upward
through emerald spires of redwood trees,
shaking cones like church bells,
past cerulean stained glass
into white light.

Sage Petals

The silk white petals of a dhoti
flutter around the stem of his body,
barely five feet above the garden.
Dew from laughter
dapples the corners of his soft eyes,
the color of Raja's Cup.
The brown earth of his sandals
sprout roots of the Bhagavad Gita
where he walks.
A wreath of rudraksha beads
drapes across the silent cadence of his heart.

Fingers shimmy on the tabla.
Small legs transform the yogi
into a lotus flower
floating on blue, quilted waves
inside a university gymnasium.
He shovels snow
from the crest of his chin with thoughtful fingers.
"I was hoping he might slip me the answer,"
says Beatle John.

Through sandalwood clouds,
I see the bounce of his shoulders
as he bubbles like children's champagne.
I offer him oranges, yellow chrysanthemums
and a white handkerchief.

Floating upon the milkweed floss of my mantra,
free-falling through a cluster of white sapphires,
pinned to a blueberry veil.
When the sky opens its shell,
a blinding pearl burns in the horizon.

I tumble through scarves of blushing grapefruit,
violet and persimmon.
I feel the dawn
lift its flaxen head into clouds.
A cardinal's serenade makes the trees shiver
as I splash into a warm pool of golden light.

JULIE'S REQUIEM

Cartwheeling across black ribbons of the city,
we shuffle the verbs and nouns of our daily lives
across the crisp, pine-scented pages of youth.
The earth rises below our feet
strewn with empty bottles
at a Trip Shakespeare concert.
We're a pair of young bohemians,
our pink and purple scarves
twirl dotted paisleys in the wind.
We laugh over Mad Libs
at the Uptown Bar in Minneapolis.

Estee Lauder's Beautiful perfume
drifts out of sunset petals.
Kitten Annabelle smells like a call girl
as she cat walks across the living room floor.
I toss the crumpled pages
of another bad day.
Your feathered words
unfurl tight fists beneath my skin.

What are the words
to change the color of your sky?
Numb and cracked, doll eyes stare
across the bone structure of your universe.
Your spine coils like a kitten
on the dark corner of the linoleum floor.

Cigarette ashes
spackle the craters of your black leather boots.
Through amber veils pebbled with ice,
you stumble over sober dreams.

Maneki Neko, your ceramic lucky charm,
crashes to the floor.
Bones slur into a trembling, watery haze
as you lean against the bar.

As your feet sink
deeper into another dimension,
I walk through a silent place,
white lilies laid across messages on stone.
Shards of memories
stained from the lingering scent
of Bacardi Rum,
cut me from the inside out.

A waterfall of white light
shimmers in the hallway
and in your brother's eyes,
illuminating the way back home.

THE ALTAR BOY FROM BUDAPEST

I.

Khrushchev's molars gnaw the countryside.
Red tanks hurl salvos from street corners,
squirting the crimson veins of Hungary
into the Danube.
A heavy machine gun clatters Russian expletives.
A Hungarian patriot opens his heart
to an iron shell,
a vapor of wings.
Under a steel roof of Soviet planes,
mortars fire without conscience,
homes explode into lumberyards,
and a boy of seven
waits to be carried 15 feet across a deep river
into Austrian marshland.
Dodging searchlights
and migrating through two minefields
in freezing rain and snow,
only the dye from his red knit cap
drips down his cheeks.
He defuses the bomb in his mother's eyes
with soft, hand-held words: "aggodj anyukam,"
"it's alright, mommy."

II.

Your feet become wings
as you grow into hiking boots.
With memories carved into the walls of our house,
I ride my scooter
back to moments from any ordinary day.
Sometimes you let me listen through the door . . .

out of a vinyl moon,
"Because," "Out In The Country,"
and "All Day And All Of The Night,"
open the soft edges of our silent moments.
We eat a bowl of Grape Nuts,
discuss vitamins and Euell Gibbons,
then shuffle a deck of paper leaves across the table.

We share DNA
and a love for trees.
We hike through archways of birch and aspen,
dodging buckthorns and stopping in the pathless wood
to watch new snow add biceps to branches.
Through silver breath clouds of a daydream,
you'll design hedges of hawthorn
and a garland of hemlock along a fast, cold stream.
My paintbrush will follow your hands.

The moon casts a shadow over your hazel eyes.
I'm locked outside your closed door,
where light enters through the crack.

You stand under a raft of cumulus clouds
that paddle across a basin of lavender sky.
Wild geraniums bloom around your knees.
The red maple tree becomes a neighborhood housing project
for chickadees and woodpeckers.
Underneath the pine tree,
a rabbit burrows into your thoughts
with eyes big as questions.

Let people whirl their sirens.
You breathe between footprints along the sodden trail,
never missing the annual flight of Canadian geese.
Once bound for priesthood,
at last you've found sanctuary
among the pine trees,
doves murmuring prayers in the cathedral.
Windswept, the scents of balsam and hemlock
draw you to the quiet ripple of a sermon.

An evangelical silence fills the woods.
A young boy raises his arms toward heaven.
The slender reeds of his fingers nest a tiny vireo
he offers upon the white altar of an apple blossom.
Healed wings release themselves
into a cloud of feathered angels.

Moonlight Lullaby

I lay my dreams
upon the pillow of your body.
Under the velvet eyelid of sky,
I watch you weave rose petals into arias
on the summer stage in Budapest.
An hourglass in the distance,
a cleft in the gravel road,
you trade your voice for an apron,
as cheeks melt together
across wafers of moonlight
to Glenn Miller.

The swirling, blue Atlantic
pulls back a rippled page of a new language,
where buffaloes once hung their bearded skulls
beneath cerulean sky.
You seek refuge there from Nikita's left fist.
Landmines become suburban backyards with outdoor grills.
Family reunions confined on onion skin stamped "Magyar Posta".
The opera house, outdoor markets
and 3am walks through the city,
are replaced by Elvis,
waxed fruit,
and home security systems.

Green lace of oak trees
beaded with cardinals and yellow finch,
rustle their petticoats in a wind dance
outside our green and white stucco house.
The aroma of chicken paprikash bubbling in the kitchen
clings to the fabric of my childhood.
Julian Bream strums out of a phonograph

as molecular lives vibrate between the walls,
catalysts in the arteries of a home.

The soft, blue scarves of your voice
wrap around my afternoon dreams like lullabies.
Pressing the guitar's ivory skin to your bosom,
small fingers pluck silver threads
that weave its music
from a homesick heart.

Early morning pours a cool pitcher of fresh air
into our skin,
where the earth rises and falls
at a farmhouse in Wisconsin.
We slip hay and apple
into the black velvet purse of a quarter horse.
I feel his heartbeat against my left thigh,
while an audience of cows
waits for us to catch their stares.

Sipping conversations in the kitchen,
we drain hours of Nescafe and Ovaltine
until the MGM lion roars.

The quiet hum of Shadows on the Moon
swaddles me with soft polka dots.
The weight of my small, but full-grown body,
hurts your knees.
My feet don't know where to put themselves
except in front of each other.
I know I must bury the placenta
and grow outside your womb.
But how I still need you
to carry me.

Burning Leaves

I.

Behind the sultry leaves of a red tulip tree,
the mellifluous trill of a blue crowned motmot.
Hovering on stilts in his tiny thatched hut,
a Mayan with broad forehead
sheathes his prayers inside a cornhusk,
releasing them through his breath.

On the island of Guanahani,
a Genoese explorer sits with an Arawak,
sipping smoke through a pronged reed.

Along the streets of Laredo,
sumac leaves and dogwood bark mingle.
Through a long-stemmed calumet,
stratus clouds form over rain dancers.

You ignite another Marlboro
around a campfire.
The Wisconsin sky inhales the thickening air
as we sit hypnotized by the flames.

II.

The quiet ashes fall and scatter like dry snow
on concrete steps of our brick house.
Smoke funnels from your nostrils.
A swell of gray wafts into the wind
through the crack of an open door.

A wrinkled brow, a squint of thought,
a trail of smoke lifts into meditation.

Withdrawn into your private world,
you climb past breathing aspen,
russet wings of a brown thrasher
carry your sapphire eyes
over beluga whales
through the tangelo sky,
lingering among invisible stars.

I reach for your fingers,
as when I first came into this world.
Fingers that clutch so many cigarettes
for so many years, only to get burned.
You never want for anything
except another cigarette.
Smoking yourself into a jail.

After supper,
we chat among the tiny bats and crickets.
As you draw at the flame for thoughts,
the quiet hiss of burning tobacco
cracks the isinglass of silence.
You tell the donkey story again,
the comic wisdom of Freddy the Freeloader,
unfolding blue petals of an esoteric garden.
Each word carries your locomotive breath.
The familiar ebb and flow glow
is the light of an oncoming train.

III.

Caught in a miasmic fog,
a cold, leaded fist
clenches my stomach
as you snatch just one more.
Another fleck of ash
into the urn.

Morning coughs paint a honeycomb
of cigarette burns inside your chest.
With the last bit of ash to sigh into its brass bed,
you crush the final soldier
into the smoldering ruins of a lost empire.

Swirling leaves of poetry
dangle between your fingers.
We observe a family of bunnies
at a rest stop.
The scrolls of our moments
carried everywhere you breathe,
huddled in shiny packages
to be taken out like books and savored slowly,
only to be burned to ash
and casually tossed into the street,
crushed under a heel.

Seeking a soft place to fall,
I follow a speckled trail of Benson & Hedges.
But I don't see you standing at the open doorway
with your cup of Taster's Choice and cigarette,
fresh from an afternoon nap.
Only a last trembling spire hangs in the air.
At last I find you under the big oak tree,
scattered like dry snow on a very cold day.

Caught In A Rainstorm

I breathe between her wings.
My heart grows inside of her.
She cracks my shell
with the warmth of her hazel eyes,
the first time anyone smiled at me.

As the sky furrows its brow,
periwinkle and rose drain from its cheek,
smudging the landscape
from emerald to slate gray.
Rain through my open window:
"He promised me I'd go first.
That sonavagun left me!"

As the moon lifts its head
over silver ripples of a final dream,
she drags her frail body across the shadows,
trying to ignore the ache
beneath her ribcage.
She folds her wings
over yellowed edges of a memory,
feet sinking deeper into the fertile urn.
As the black bones of trees disappear,
I hear your whistled flight
fade into rising veils of scarlet, coral and violet.

When I could breathe inside an egg,
I never felt the size of the world
until now.

Homeless Wind

Under a black veil,
white fire forks through saturated sky.
The day hangs like wet wool.
Thoughts stick together like mud:
 "Ten more minutes and then you can miss me."
 "If anything should happen to me..."
 "I will always love you no matter what happens."

I think of you lying there
counting each breath,
slowly drowning inside your chest.
A misty shadow sits across my eyes,
hiding from salivating stares.
How much longer
before my soul gets off its knees
and you are there?

The hands that planted marigolds
in the windowsills of my eyes,
have become ashes inside a small, cardboard box.
Arms that lifted me into the stars,
sieve through my fingers as light.
When your wings surrendered
to the blue tourmaline sky of your eyes,
I heard my name
rustle through the aspen leaves.

Below cirrus angels,
you slowly lift your head.
The sky cracks like an egg,
releasing its yolk across the horizon.
As the black fleece of night shrinks back,

you touch the meadow with golden fire.
Daffodils lean against your beams.

An old cat slowly shrinks into her bones,
a smoldering shadow across the sidewalk
nobody wants,
finally stops shivering.
Plate glass windows open in the east.
Some scarred from too much rain,
some broken and gaping from hurled stones,
leaving behind their sharp edges.

Roots under my feet,
I can only watch
as evening above my shoulders
swallows you.

I weave past human bodies,
sifting through maple leaves,
fluttering about on homeless feet,
listening for the sound of my name.

Sanctuary

The sun opens its silk-screen fan
of rose, tangerine and fuchsia
behind the grassy edge of chessboard fields.
Your arms slowly lift into the clouds.
From the sable brush of a cardinal's throat,
a watercolor of love songs
across the Bristol board of blue sky.

The sun releases its golden oil
through your lace curtains.
It splatters across Chinese landscapes
hung on aging walls,
rubs the bronze feet of Buddha,
balms the marbled lips of Guan Shi Yin.

The scent of you
lingers like a mist in the air.
It settles upon the dried flowers and ginger jars,
the copper coins tossed into I Ching hexagrams,
in the empty chair of your writing desk,
over LP jackets and chatter of books.
I bury my face in the multi-colored bathrobe
that echoes with the memory of lavender
and water music.

In the rocking chair of a reverie,
your hair absorbs the moonlight.
Under the beaded parasol of sky
where a full moon lactates
across the gray Berber rug,
its long, silver arms
guide you through the loneliness.

Where your soul bends its knees
for every songbird,
housecat
and human you have ever loved,
from this sliver of earth
where you surrender to the unconscious night
one last time,
the feathers of your dreams
become your wings.

My Father's Voice Is In The Trees

The tangerine sun
reaches into the open arms of sky,
spilling across the alfalfa fields.
It flows through my veins
until I am filled with light.

Emerald leaves flutter under your breath,
shimmering in sunlight.
Your roots are a labyrinth
in the beating earth of my heart.
I hear your voice in the rings
of an oak tree,
touching the knobs and grooves of familiar limbs
that I used to climb.
I feel your sap flow through my skin
until I, too, grow wild with leaves.

"Rustle Of Spring" piano concerto
tumbles from your fingers,
as cardinals, nuthatches and chickadees
flutter between the keys,
before scattering
across lavender fields of sky.
The sun lays its flaxen head
upon your ruffled shoulders
while other trees try to touch you.

I could always lean against you,
but you've taught me to look up
if I want to see petals of light
shimmering through the dark leaves of the forest.

Years stretch your skin into the marbled sky.
As the wind tosses you in every direction,
you sigh more easily these days.
Suddenly, the birds have become silent.

My heart, a frightened sparrow
shook out of its tree,
swallowed by the deep throat of night,
searching for moonlight between the shadows.

METAMORPHOSIS

One mile below the heartbeat
of a circling hawk,
winds shapeshift stones into totem animals.

She empties the red petals of her youth
into the parched throat of earth.
Will she open what's left of her
to the light?

She wipes morning dew from a heated brow,
curving space with her expanding body.
Lemon talc flecked with pearls
dusts her soul.
Monarch wings flutter around her chest.
Has time lost its nectar?

Unfurling melodies,
poetry and a hunger to bring back the trees
fill her barren womb.
Translucent fingertips of a concerto
almost fully formed
shimmer in an amniotic bowl,
words leaving her body
catching light.

When fractals of snow
fall upon the bones of alley cats,
her robe of leaves begins to dry—
velvet edges of her shadow curl inward.

A northeast wind shivers
under the white wing of a snow goose,
lifting her spirit from its green cage,
glissading above the empty trees
to carry her home.

On Stained Glass Wings

Between Earth and Moon,
I dive through white light
glittered with fireflies.
Privacy without walls,
human judgement lacks oxygen here.
A crown of seven angels
shimmer around the stubborn head of Taurus,
street lights along the freeway to God.
In the liquid silence,
stars shake like tiny bells
against the winds of Neptune.

Galloping on Sagittarius
through a hologram of twenty dimensions,
I vault over a waterfall of shooting stars.

The silver moons shrink from memory.
Stars vanish into themselves.
My stained glass wings
flutter through white scarves.
The skylight over the universe
brightens as I get closer.
Like the yellow glow of a farmhouse window
that lies awake waiting,
the other side of loneliness
illuminates the miles home.

Pas de Deux

I.

If God has a uterus, twin flames ignite
inside the soft membrane walls of an egg.
The wild, smoky shapes of their longing
pirouette across green fire.
As she leaps to his desires,
he lifts her over the waterfall.
A wreath of trees around them waffle the sky.
Crystal leaves dapple a running stream.
Dawn opens its throat
with the liquid flute of a cardinal,
in the pillow talk of pine trees.

She longs to spoon
the sweet yellow custard of the moment,
following the scent of lilacs.
A cloud of white feathers
billows from her tiny waist.
Her long neck winds around his
like a wedding ring.
She finds the sky in his arms
before he releases her,
a slippered toe still pointing in his direction.

II.

I'm free falling through the jagged teeth of civilization.
You walk across the words of this poem,
but where are you on the map?
Your voice, my compass.
But I somehow lost the frequency
along the mountains of my mother's thighs.

The pink petals of my toes
twirl across cornfields, lacquer floors,
on wooded hiking trails near the big lake,
searching for the summit of your shoulders.
I know I'm home
when the photosphere of your grey eyes
answers mine.
As the pages of my years begin to amber,
every chapter draws me closer
to the sound of your breathing.

III.

As morning glories fold into themselves
under the broken moon,
hands thin as a dream
grab mine.
You find the spaces between my fingers
and fill them with yours.
I cleave to this moment like a wren to wind,
until the shotgun of my alarm clock
shatters the wispy images
of your umber hair and brooding face.
I wear the shrapnel of your absence.

IV.

Under a shimmering beam of white light,
two spirits reunite
along the rocky shore,
where lilies of the valley grow,
and a flute concerto plays in the trees.

BOUQUET OF WEEDS

Reverence bends at the knees
under the tall steeple of an olive tree.
A woman wearing long chestnut hair,
rouge, and a scarlet dress,
aches to touch Him
from the inside out.
She strokes His feet with spikenard oil,
and scatters petals
of white orchid, saffron crocus and kadupul.

The crowd girdles Him
like ants around sweet tree sap.
He carries a crippled child,
an old woman
and a beaten dog.

The dry Mediterranean sands
cling to my bare feet
that carry memories like old stories.
I gather milkweed pods, cattails and dandelions,
placing them into His hands.

He bandages my loneliness with warm flesh.
Soft folds of white light
drape over His shoulders
as I sink into the wet russet earth of His eyes
that pull me out of the shadows,
refracting through the etched glass of my heart
until it shatters.

SENTINEL OF LIGHT

Fractals of rose light
shimmer through a trellis of maple leaves.
Its pink paws catwalk across the underbrush.
Green ruffled pantaloons
around the bristled thigh of an oak,
where white doves lift out of feathered dreams.
The forest carries my feet deep into its ribcage,
digesting hoof prints.
Violets bloom along the soft edges
of a fast beating heart,
somewhere between calm and shivering.

My universe snaps
under a heavy rubber heel.
Velvet ears swivel toward a spasm in the shoulder of the forest.
The part of me still wearing white spots
crouches in the tall grass.
Two sets of tracks pockmark the earth
as fear pulls me out of a dream
into only memory of trees.

As mouths fill with bullets,
I outrun their eyes,
limping across the violets.
I remembered to breathe
on the other side of a dark hill
rippled with clover and wildflowers,
brushing the billowed skirts of angels.

Pine trees release their incense
into the sanctuary.
Perched in the emerald choir loft,
a hosanna of cardinals
glorify a beautiful day.
Bumblebees hum benediction
over cornflower, chamomile
and red poppy.
The verdant cathedral shimmers in petaled water
as golden cowslip bow their heads.

A white wing of light
explodes across the stained-glass sky,
draping over trembling shoulders.

A New Day

The sky opens its fiery heart
behind an arrow of black trees.
Swirling fingers of pastel yellow,
fuschia and apricot
shuffle the rippled deck of clouds.
A froth of pink bubbles
rises to the top.
Feeling the pulse of a new day,
morning glories open their pearled cheeks
to the crimson light.
My thin feet
grip around a sunbeam nodding in the breeze,
needled bough catches fire.
Nectar pours from my throat with psalms.
As my soul lifts upward with the sun,
I open my red wings,
carrying the breath of the Creator.

About the Author

Angel Elisa Collier makes her debut as a writer with her first book of poetry, *The Zen of Falling Leaves*. For several years, she has studied under the direction of poet and author Diane Frank. Angel is the recipient of the H. Edward Cannon Memorial Award for the poem "Polonaise for Chopin." She grew up among the woods and rolling hills of Minnesota and Wisconsin. She received her B.A. in Art at Maharishi University in Fairfield, Iowa, where she currently resides.

For further information, contact:

E-mail: le_fleur@kittymail.com
Address: Angel Collier
P.O. Box 1974
Fairfield, IA 52556